comfortable
COUNTRY

comfortable COUNTRY

RYLAND
PETERS
& SMALL
LONDON NEW YORK

ENRICA STABILE

photography by **Christopher Drake**

text by **Julia Watson**

First published in the United States in 2001.
This exclusive edition published for
Direct Brands, Inc in 2009
by Ryland Peters & Small, Inc.
519 Broadway
5th Floor
New York, NY 10012

ISBN: 978-1-60751-331-5
Printed in China
www.rylandpeters.com

Designer **Vicky Holmes**
Senior Editor **Clare Double**
Location and Picture Research Manager
Kate Brunt
Location Researcher **Sarah Hepworth**
Production **Patricia Harrington**
Art Director **Gabriella Le Grazie**
Publishing Director **Alison Starling**

European Locations **Enrica Stabile**

Front cover and back jacket above right
and left, designer Barbara Davis' own
house in upstate New York.

Library of Congress Cataloging-in-Publication Data for first edition

Stabile, Enrica.
    Comfortable country : peaceful homes inspired by the country / Enrica Stabile ;
photography by Christopher Drake.
       p. cm.
    Includes index.
    ISBN 1-84172-202-2
    1. Interior decoration--United States--History--20th century. 2. Decoration and
ornament, Rustic--United States--History--20th century. I. Title.

NK2004 .S74 2001
747.213'09'04--dc21

                                                                                                    2001031879

contents

an introduction to comfortable country

To me, comfort is almost synonymous with country. I don't mean the comfort of a large, air-conditioned home, containing all the latest electrical goods. To be at ease, you need something different. Country is not simply an area you can find on a map, it is a place of the spirit. Even the simplest home in the country can be like heaven. Comfortable country style is not just about owning a house on a hill, on the edge of a wood in the mountains, on a cliff, or on a sandy beach at the seaside. It is about a different way of living, more simply and peacefully, as time passes.

I would like to share my recipe for wellbeing. Leave town, go to a place you love and that is important to you, and look carefully around you at the smallest details: a blade of grass, a ladybug on the windowsill, or a ray of sunlight coming through the windows, lighting thousands of tiny dust particles. Sit outside and refresh your mind with this wonderful place. Unlike a town apartment, even a simple, almost spartan retreat has a different view from each side, and the view constantly changes according to the light, the season, and the time of day. Inside, objects brought from town look different: often they are not merely decorative, but regain their inherent qualities. The simplest piece of furniture will assert its unique personality: a bed, a chair, a glass holding a flower from the garden–simple elements, but together they create a harmony of style that is inviting, relaxed, and comfortable to live with.

Notice the happiness of a visit to the country. Friends know they will spend peaceful hours relaxing in front of a crackling fire, sunk into a comfortable old sofa, around a pine table waiting to savor a delicious meal, or outside in the shade of an arbor. They will remember the feel of natural materials like wood, stone, and leather, and the soft colors that make the atmosphere so inviting. Each moment shared together in these surroundings will stay in their minds as a precious memory. If you do not own a country retreat, think about nature in your urban home. Slow down to a quieter rhythm, focus on the changing seasons, and try to create an inviting and peaceful atmosphere. Use simple materials to make your interiors naturally elegant, with a combination of beautiful utilitarian objects and treasured country-style antiques. Your home will always be ready to welcome you with warmth and friendliness, and an atmosphere of complete wellbeing.

Opposite top left This corner epitomizes comfortable country style: a calm, peaceful atmosphere created by beautiful pale paint and touches of natural wicker, cloth, and wool. The painted armoire houses bedroom linen, scented with lavender sachets, while the casual garden chair is an informal touch.

Opposite top right The purity of this simple yet romantic bedroom, with its tied voile curtain at the window, is warmed by a checked blanket.

Opposite bottom left Light streams through the tall windows of this living room, which houses an amazing collection of disparate elements including animal horns and monumental busts and urns. An elegant table holds one of a pair of white china urns.

Opposite bottom right A warm yellow entrance hall is complemented by the duck-egg blue front door. Flowers stand ready to greet visitors on a child-size chair, while a colorful rag rug leads toward the oak staircase.

country
influences

changing seasons

No one can ignore the seasons. Consciously or not, we have a physical response to them as they alter. In winter, our bodies incline toward hibernation: sweaters and blazing fires are as comforting to the spirit as to the flesh. In the heat of summer, we abandon dark clothing and adopt a more languorous existence. We turn to nature's palette below the horizon for the colors of our winter surroundings—earth, the trunks of trees, stones, and berries. In summer, our minds wander to the sun, the sea, and the clearer, lighter shades of natural warmth.

Changes in the seasons can be reflected in our rooms without upheaval. The mood is established in the details. Herald the informality of early spring with a simple glass jar of hedgerow flowers, or summer with a colorful bunch of blooms from your backyard. In the warmer seasons, take up the rugs from your floors. Remove clutter. Leave behind only those pieces you absolutely love. Clear away the ashes from an open fireplace and stow cushions, rugs, and eiderdowns—cozy barricades against the bitter chill—away in closets, trunks, and boxes until the year

open windows
and doors to admit the
springtime

Above *Don't limit yourself to conventional containers. In establishing a sense of ease, this plain mug makes a far more effective holder for a blowsy rose than a regular glass or china vase.*

Right *Two folding chairs, set casually beside a glorious perennial bed, offer a nonchalant invitation to sit and admire the flowers.*

Opposite left *Any time of year, flowers make a decorative point. In this light-filled corner, a galvanized bucket filled with an informal bunch of blue catnip picks up the color of a painted hutch and storage box.*

Opposite right *The deliberately casual mix of wildflowers with a single clematis in a glass jar on a kitchen window perfectly reflects the relaxed manner of living associated with the sun-filled days of early summer.*

This page and opposite right *A wide covered porch makes a perfect summer bedroom with outdoor shower. Lengths of white fabric draped over the bed's canopy, a breezy sail of white sheet to provide the shower's essential privacy, and a basket of towels all celebrate languid days of comfortable living.*

Opposite left *Placing the vibrant reds of summer fruits and vegetables in front of a windowbox of fresh contrasting green brings the glow of the season indoors. The diversity of the elements on the table gives the display its informality.*

turns again. In this way, rooms are unburdened and given a chance to breathe with greater lightness, in tune with the breezes that waft freely through opened windows. The pale blues of warmer skies and pinks and yellows of spring buds echo the colors in nature. Brought inside, they reflect our desire for a fresh start. As temperatures climb and days lengthen, our optimism and sense of openness are renewed.

White, the purest of hues, hums with a clarity against which all the other shades of summer will sing. Summer is the time of year for crisp white sheets, tablecloths embroidered with flowers, cushions in faded floral cottons or candy-pink stripes on white. White is imperative. Cover sofas and chairs upholstered in winter colors with damask tablecloths, or yards of muslin or voile. Their folds and pleats as you tuck them in conveys informality and ease. With white as a clean background, touches of color can be added without obscuring the freshness. But keep the

crisp white touches
are the essence of
summer

a pitcher of rushes, twigs,
and bright berries sounds a
perfect autumnal note

colors and details simple. For the best summery effect, stick to one color plus white in each room. In a blue and white room, line a pretty collection of blue spongeware dishes on top of a chest of drawers. In a white and pink one, use cushions trimmed in pink or covered in fabric of pink blossoms. Old glass bottles make an appealing display on a side table. Create displays you can change with the seasons: in winter, place pinecones, candlesticks, and colored glassware along a mantel; in summer, arrange a collection of seashells, driftwood, and stones. It's spring cleaning with the eye.

In fall and winter rooms, more than one color can be used in happy conjunction, but keep them within the same spectrum of nature; the golds, dark greens, and rich blushes of turning leaves or the grays, taupes, darker browns, and colder blues of deeper winter. Amber, plum, forest green, and sapphire also belong to fall and winter.

Above *Collections of dishes in interesting shapes or soothing colors deserve to be shown off to their best advantage. The doors of this kitchen cabinet full of richly colored Provençal plates and dishes are left open to show off a display that is easily as interesting as a carefully arranged set piece.*

Right *Stones, bronze urns, and architectural ornaments surround this white Louis XVI chest of drawers. What makes this more formal display work is the focus on the strong shapes of the sculptural elements, with the apparently casual elements, like the pebbles and the paper flower collars, restricted in color to white.*

Opposite *An exuberant display of flowers in a shining copper vat echoes those painted on the doors of the 1730s Bavarian armoire in the dining room, giving a seasonal summer lift to the mellow amber of the living room wall leading into it. As fall takes the place of summer, the flowers will give way to colorful berries and leaves. Floorboards left bare in the dining room emphasize the tranquility and airiness of the space.*

This page One key to the comfortable country look is a feeling of spontaneity in the arrangement of objects, but remember the fine line between an unforced display and untidiness. This front hall contains a number of different articles, but each has a point—in the appeal of its shape, as with the garden urns, or its usefulness to the household.

Opposite top right The French cane day bed, generous cushion, and soft throw offer a seductive inducement to settle down with a book. Behind, on the table, is a restful collage of seaweeds.

Opposite bottom right A workbasket filled with sewing and knitting materials suggests time for hobbies and peaceful household activities.

As the weather turns cold, pile rugs back on the floor, fold thickly woven blankets over the arms of sofas and chairs, and place a log basket or pile of kindling near the fireplace. Cast intimate pools of light with a variety of table lamps, instead of depending upon a striking central light source. Pull curtains against the cold and dark, and enjoy nurturing food.

These are responses to nature we can echo with ease in our surroundings. A ceramic pitcher of rushes and twigs beaded with bright berries sounds the perfect autumnal note. A voluptuous throw of nubby weaves in jeweled colors or plaids, laid across a bed or sofa, creates the perfect mood in winter. Then add piles of scatter cushions and mounds of comforting blankets, and any whisper of the bitter chill outside is banished. Whatever nature is doing outside, you can reflect it—or protect yourself against it—in your safe haven indoors.

peacefulness

In today's fast-moving world, home should be a haven of renewal; it doesn't have to be a showcase for hi-tech trends. Comfortable country style reminds us that some things are timeless. A monogrammed pillowcase brings to mind a less urgent period; a bunch of flowers on a windowsill is an encouragement to enjoy the simple beauty around us. It's an uncomplicated look. This doesn't mean it casts elegance or style aside: it is as distinctive as anything at the cutting edge of design, but far easier to live with.

Comfortable country conveys a sense of peace and harmony. Its clarity and simplicity transmit, in a contemporary setting, a seductive peacefulness that contrasts with blowsy chintzes and tassels. It is as classic as a brocades-and-silk style, but aims to enfold us in serenity and ease.

Opposite In this almost monastically uncluttered guest bedroom, decoration is freely established in the same understated way by the carved green decoration above the bed and the green silk cover upon it. Crisp white linen on plump pillows and soft piles of wool sweaters, blankets, or throws left neatly exposed on shelves convey a subliminal message of comfort and security while looking alluring.

This page To generate a sense of peacefulness in any room, keep each of its elements clear. Restrict the color palette, control clutter, allow the space to breathe. In this French bedroom, the only pattern to break the white of the walls, plain curtains, bed linen, and cushion fabric is the delicate print on the quilt. This allows the distinctive line of the crapaud (toad) armchair's iron frame to make a decorative impact.

This page Apart from white, green is known to be the most restful color to live with. Here a breezy shade of spearmint paint is applied to the porch floor of this elegant Long Island retreat, as well as to the swing. By uniting the two with color, decorative diversions can be made without jarring the eye, as in the use of a medley of materials for the cushions.

Opposite Giving house-room to this white marbled-topped iron garden table is an inspiration that adds a deliberately unceremonious note to a country living room where white is one of the key colors. A reminder of its outdoor origins is given by the white-painted metal basket containing a rich but almost haphazard display of roses. Behind is a painted rose trellis.

an uncomplicated
scene set apart from a busy life is
a retreat

Clarity is the guide. Each household item and piece of furniture should count as useful or comfortable. With this idea at its heart, home becomes a placid retreat from the outside world, created from simple elements. Restrict color schemes to one or two per room, and limit patterns to cushions or throws.

Gingham, stripes, ticking, or faded florals on tea-stained backgrounds are all redolent of old-fashioned charm and imbue a room with a sense of peace. They can provide a perfect foil for a diverse range of furniture from any period, toning down hard edges. Use these traditional materials with equal effect at windows, on chairs and sofas, and to cover pillows. To give strong-colored ticking a softer look, turn it inside out.

An eclectic collection of pottery pots on a side table, simple green and white china on tea-time trays, or a row of pegs hung with shawls and scarves all offer calmness and serenity. We sense their message of domestic peace. They evoke a time when home was a sanctuary and decoration was not designed to dramatize or excite; it existed as a restorative background to daily life. Simple displays, emphasizing the activities of the household, are as effective today in city or country settings. Try an armoire casually stacked with an assortment of china (in the same or coordinated colors or it will simply look messy). With linens, you can heap several piles of different colors, as long as each pile is the same color throughout—or again you will merely create a jumble. Sets of linen tied with ribbons like birthday presents convey country charm.

If you have high ceilings, remember the tops of cabinets and armoires, where you can show off an orderly stack of pretty blankets, a collection of hatboxes, or old leather suitcases. Exposing these personal objects creates a mood of comfort and tranquility.

Even formal set pieces can convey simplicity, if the components accord—the placing of a glass ornament or vase upon a white-painted desk or side table, perhaps under a mercuried mirror, each article mimicking the essence of the other. This is at the heart of Gustavian style, so much part of the serenity of Swedish country houses. It captures a

This page Natural light is a decorative element that lifts the spirits. Take advantage of it. It costs absolutely nothing and can be used in a number of ways. To suggest space, emphasize or frame incoming light with white or pale paint. Or place a chair where light floods in, to draw attention to its presence and make the most of it in comfort.

Opposite To bring brilliance into a room, arrange attractive pieces of glass on tabletops where they can reflect the source of light. Thrift-store or yard-sale finds of glass perfume bottles, pitchers, and bowls make a pretty display. Decanters no longer in use in the dining room can take on a new role accentuating light coming in from a window.

This page *The feeling of calm in this upstairs corridor comes from the light pouring in from two large skylights. The temptation to fill the space with tables and other furniture often found in halls has been resisted. Only a slatted chair, wall sconces, and modest decorations interrupt this spacious passage.*

Opposite *With tremendous aplomb, this living room window has been hung with printed voile curtains in two colors that echo the freshness of the yard beyond. Floating airily inside an extremely formal draped valance, they add a touch of frivolity to an otherwise serious piece of decoration.*

soothing stillness in pared-down details, pale painted furniture, and walls and floors all washed in the same continuous color. All these elements are part of comfortable country style today.

Old-fashioned paint finishes such as distemper, flat oil paint, limewash, or casein milk paint, often tinted with the soft hues of natural pigments, can still be used to good effect. Distemper, which gives a pleasantly chalky finish, was once popular for covering poor plaster walls, yet flatters today's smoother surfaces. Limewash, best brushed onto lime plaster, gives an elegant flat, stony finish. However, it won't work over modern latex. Flat oil paint offers a very flat finish and looks good on woodwork, but marks easily. Oil eggshell is a practical alternative since it marks less, but it does have a slight sheen. These washes and paints, along with natural pigments, are once more available from discerning paint suppliers and mixers, to create unique colors and finishes.

Accessibility is the basis of comfortable country appeal. A glut of pattern and texture is visually indigestible, discouraging a sense of ease, and its opposite, minimalism, demands that the things we like to have about us—books, a piece of sewing—should be cleared away in order not to disturb the clean lines of the style. The intrinsic peacefulness in comfortable country includes accepting the restful ebb and flow of life.

nostalgia

Right Comfortable country style offers a look where treasured keepsakes from childhood or pretty items collected at antique fairs can fit happily. Give pride of place to an old wooden plaything that is as attractive in its craftsmanship as in the sentiment it evokes. Its positioning next to a wood-columned mantelpiece and walls of a similar color is perfect.

Opposite It is the country flowers of Victorian storybooks, not the architectural blooms of exotic jungles, that make for a gently nostalgic mood. Whether part of the embroidered design on a tablecloth found in a yard sale, or plunged fresh from the field into a rustic pitcher, flowers strike an essential chord. Look out for floral motifs in thrift stores, imprinted upon a set of farmhouse tableware. Contrast florals with stripes—a juxtaposition long practiced by interior designers.

Below A prettily monogrammed pillow is highlighted upon an old rush-seated chair—classic white on white.

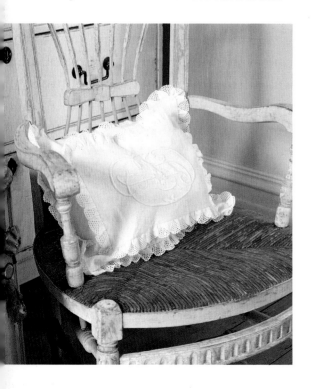

Somewhere in everyone's imagination is a place where easygoing afternoons ended with golden cake and preserves full of fruit, and where sprigged eiderdowns and faded quilts bulged on beds in lavender-scented rooms. Where time ran more slowly and summers were warm, the sweet smell of newmown lawns filled the air, and bees buzzed in flowerbeds.

This image recalls a time when all appeared safe and ordered, and routines seemed set from one year to the next, from beach sand in the sandwiches to hand-knitted scarves wound around winter necks. A jack-o-lantern time, with drifts of drying leaves to kick, and hot chocolate to come home to; a bugs-in-jars time, with daisy chains to weave.

Opposite The wit of the metalwork chandelier adds a frivolous touch to a restful kitchen. The leisurely mood is conveyed by the idiosyncratic collection of pottery pitchers along the shelf and the wall sconces above the kitchen counter.

Above right Cooking ingredients don't have to be hidden. Store them on open shelves in containers in pottery and tin, more pleasing than standard glass jars. The pitchers above are not just for display.

Below right Old French enamel containers are finding their way across to antique stores in the United States. A border of patterned or laced paper, or embroidered fabric, pinned along the shelf, borrows effectively from the past.

The gleam of polished wood, the scent of vanilla, the crunch of frost underfoot: even now these sights, smells, and sounds evoke an age when there was always time to crumble lavender into a bowl, to stare at logs crackling in the grate, to gather baskets of berries and pick flowers. Time, too, to hang out linen to catch gusts of air among its folds, and store it carefully in a warm closet, with oranges stuck with cloves or pomanders between the sheets.

Memory is a capricious faculty. The sight of a yellowing luggage tag or faded bundle of ribbons can remind us of a period that might not even have been our own. Such thoughts don't need to come from personal experience. What matters is the way we can respond to them. Nostalgia is no less poignant for being a brief encounter with someone else's past. Its flavor is worth recapturing for the sense of comfort and simplicity it brings.

In these times of mass manufacture, mass marketing, and mass media, we miss the intimacy of the past, the sense of contact with something personal that is conveyed by a piece of handworked lace or the embroidered edge of a rough cotton cloth. Details like these map out the hours when some unknown hand worked diligently at their design. A kitchen pot, its enamel lightly chipped, conjures up floral aprons and sensible hands at a scrubbed wooden table forming the structure of a family meal, while a row of pitchers along a shelf evokes the soothing smell of fresh milk. With the right pieces, you can recreate similar images quite simply. Make a start by scenting your linen cupboards with lavender bags or bars of gloriously fragranced soap. Even hand towels piled on a simple wooden chair suggest a leisurely and more comfortable existence.

We have become too quick to throw away and replace. Before you abandon that basket whose willow may have unraveled around the rim, or throw out that empty jelly jar, consider if it offers the possibility of another role. Set by the front door, the basket might be just the place for gloves that separate themselves in drawers, house keys, dog leashes, and other essentials that jumble up in entrance halls. A row of glass jars along a bathroom windowsill or shelf could hold toothbrushes, tubes of toothpaste, or colored ends of soap. Suddenly these things cease to be irritants you can't wait to discard, and take on an interest of their own.

Many of us own treasures from a past when languid afternoons and longer evenings were spent in embroidery, quilting, lace, and needlework. All we need to do is raid our family attics, trunks, and boxes to uncover it. If these items truly have been discarded, then hunt where others' treasure has been banished, in garage sales, yard sales, thrift stores, and flea markets.

Opposite *Bold fabric adds a romantic flourish above a painted French Directoire bed. The rag rug has been picked for its soft shades that echo the American quilt.*

Above left *A pile of antique boxes, covered with faded fabric prints and redolent of history, brings a sentimental link with the past to a contemporary bedside table.*

Below left *The beautifully monogrammed towel and the pretty china bowl of soaps it is resting beneath connect to an age when spare time was usefully spent with needle and thread.*

recapture the
unassuming style of a contented era
not so long ago

A country-style look with a touch of nostalgia is easy to create. Simplicity is the key. Use pale paint and washes on walls; wallpaper suggests formal receiving rooms. Give table lamps shades of plain or painted parchment, or a gathering of simply patterned fabric. Add rugs in rounds or rectangles of hook-worked pieces from the scrap bag—an informal mix of colors, patterns, and textures. Mats of heavy wools, pulled in patterns through sackcloth backing, or rag rugs in colored stripes of rough ripped cloth, are cottage coverings still easy to find. Curtains found in thrift stores and yard sales, faded at the edges; a pile of sweaters in soft earthy shades piled upon a wooden stool; an old basketweave chair half-draped with a blanket: uncomplicated things such as these convey the comfort and ease of simple country style. In fact, it takes little more than a faded quilt tossed over a modern sofa, a collection of pottery and china vases along a shelf, or a display of woven baskets, old fabric-covered boxes, or *objets trouvés* that come with a history of long and fond usage to cast a country mood over a carefully contrived modern urban living room.

It's a style entirely open to personal interpretation and so can work happily with contemporary pieces. A mellow leather hatbox is for one person a place to store outdoor shoes, for another a useful place to keep bedside books. An old meat locker is just the thing for bathroom lotions, or dishcloths and napkins in a kitchen corner. Country style reflects a time before mass production, before factory outpourings of copy upon copy of identical items made uniqueness scarce. It's a personal affair, an individual reaction to individual things.

Take nature as your cue for colors and materials. The style is modest. Silks, ruffles, and furbelows are best left for a grander stage. Comfortable country homes are content with cotton and wool, gentle ruffles, and ribbon. The

Left *A young girl's bedroom is filled with romantic objects and designs inspired by the past. Yet the look is fresh, not gloomy, achieved through emphasizing the delicacy of its lines in white. The color is used profusely—in the cloth that covers the bedside table, as the background of the sprigged cotton quilt, and on the tongue-and-groove paneling. Even the iron bed's elaborate curlicued frame is lightened with white paint. The airiness continues in a chair that is not solid and upholstered, but white-painted wood and cane.*

Right and opposite above *Old silver-topped glass perfume bottles add a pretty touch to a plain side table.*

Opposite below *Pillows on the bed are a feminine mix of ruffles and lace, gathers and embroidery, that reflects a bygone time.*

everyday country kitchenware of past generations was rarely decorated. In France, Italy, and Spain, local pottery plates and dishes, often with fluted or scalloped edges, were fired in deep hues of amber, green, blue, and terracotta. In England and in North America, paler colors were in more common use, but shapes were still simple. Even more formal dining china and faience was only modestly decorated, by hand or transfer, with floral patterns or country landscape scenes in muted blue, brown, or burgundy.

Fabric makes a statement. All manner of sources can be explored to find interesting cloth that adds focus to rooms and the pieces of furniture within them. Just one length of an old textile can successfully establish the whole look.

Embroidering, appliqué, and quilting have been part of domestic life across continents for centuries. In North America especially, quilts tell stories and, through their patterning, can sometimes reveal where they were made. Such treasures can still be unearthed in attics and antique stores. Pieces like these are generally affordable and are deeply rewarding to use. The printed color of an old quilt may have been muted to faded shades of pink, lavender, and fern green, tones that no modern manufacturer can hope to reproduce.

When technology became a fact of life we had to assimilate, many of us turned to minimalism and a pared-down style to reflect the proficiency of our new world. But real people are not suited to behaving as though daily life were a laboratory experiment—cool, clean, and clinical. Efficiency has its place, but in the things that we choose to live with we need an intimacy and a softness to keep us gentle, and to keep us human.

Opposite Old French farmhouse armoires were popular in country rooms for displaying special china. Here, pretty blue-painted pottery is stacked in a casual fashion that removes any pomposity from the collection. It is an appealing look that is easily emulated with contemporary cabinets; remove center panels from the cabinet doors and replace them with chicken wire.

Above The pieces in the collection do not all come from the same set, which adds to the charm of the display. But they are all the same shade of blue, which keeps the group from looking messy. It is important not to give the impression that the pieces have been set down with any particular symmetry—it is precisely in its informality that the display works.

utility

The practical essentials of life need not be unattractive simply because they are useful. There can be such pleasure in the sight of a pile of linen, or a cluster of utensils in a pot. In traditional country homes, the business of running a household was visible. This didn't mean there was no room for charm and making things look their best. The appeal of comfortable country style is that it makes artful use of simple effects to create an unpretentious, relaxing look. Unassuming things—an antique pine washstand with a pretty china water pitcher, or embroidered cotton towels in the bathroom—inspire a sense of comfort we instantly respond to.

The details to borrow are modest. Cupboards and kitchen shelves might be lined with wallpaper or edged in a paper border; patterned tiles used to catch splashes behind sinks and bathtubs. Try colorful French-style faience designs of country scenes, deep blue Delft tiles, or Moorish-influenced Portuguese and Spanish tiles in strong blues, sharp greens with yellow, or varied shades of crimson. In addition, old Victorian tiles are still plentiful, and popular, in the United States and Britain.

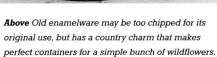

Above *Old enamelware may be too chipped for its original use, but has a country charm that makes perfect containers for a simple bunch of wildflowers.*

Left *The ceramic sink in this kitchen has not yet been plumbed in, but it is in full use, with a bucket beneath to catch waste water. From the galvanized trash can to the doweling dish drainer on the wall, much has been made of natural materials to establish a naive and unpretentious look in this simple kitchen corner.*

Opposite above left *An old-fashioned egg box in a cool larder, set on a marble slab, stores fresh farm eggs. Egg boxes such as these sometimes appear in mail order catalogs. Best for storing newly gathered eggs for a short time, they must be kept in a cool place.*

Opposite below left *A wide, shallow, china-clay farmhouse sink is the perfect scullery basin for cutting and soaking cut flowers, cleaning paintbrushes and leafy vegetables, scaling fish, and other household chores. Once collectors' items, they are now common currency at most kitchen suppliers. Exposed pipes add to the rustic charm of this informal room.*

Opposite right *A collection of sun-faded linens makes a pretty public pile on a kitchen sideboard or table.*

This page *This idiosyncratic kitchen demonstrates how happily several styles can work together. The retro 1950s kitchen unit with ingenious cupboards, compartments, and roll-top bread box proves that furniture which functions effectively is never long out of fashion. High cream gloss paint and the refrigerator door handles (find imitations among the supplies of good hardware stores) are stylish details to copy.*

Opposite *Despite its modern burners and electric oven, this kitchen has a comfortable country look. A haphazard mixing of materials and levels—marble beneath the naïf patterned tiles, the sink set higher than the cooking zone, the café curtains hiding the plumbing, and the collection of utensils and pieces of china on the two rustic shelves—tempers any suggestion of modernity conveyed by the two-piece cooking arrangement.*

This page This high-ceilinged, light-filled space makes a utility room that is charming enough to take extra guests. A thick blanket covered by a pretty cloth makes the perfect ironing board. Period lights and galvanized buckets help imbue the room with the relaxed feel of a bygone age. Blue on the table, window frame, and patterned border around the bed dilutes the room's functional look.

Opposite left Concrete softened with a yellow tint forms the counter for a drop-in stainless-steel sink.

Opposite top right Dinner plates piled on a white hutch create a relaxed look.

Opposite bottom right This well-stocked china cupboard sets a comfortable mood while providing practical storage.

Color-sponged or painted enameled tins, traditional storage in France, Germany, and North America, and tall round wooden boxes from Russian dacha kitchens, with leaflike patterns in yellow, green, and red, can be found in thrift and antique stores.

Copy country housewives of times gone by when there weren't such aids to neatness as modern knife blocks and utensil racks. Bunch ladles, whisks, and spoons together in a jug or crock, within easy reach of the stove or sink. Countertops are a modern device. With comfortable country style, a scrubbed pine table can become a work surface that is as practical as it is esthetically pleasing. Store essential supplies, like plastic bottles of cleaning products, trash cans, and old cloths, under a freestanding or ceramic sink behind a simple curtain hung along a wire.

Curtains gathered at top and bottom look pretty behind the glazed fronts of cabinets hiding dishes or household linen in more formal rooms. White curtains in a white-painted cabinet look particularly effective. Heavy curtains hanging over doors that lead outside guard against seeping winter drafts (even if you

Opposite *Storage is easy in comfortable country homes: simply pick what looks pretty and relaxed. In this kitchen, flatware is sorted into different pots and jars, and serving dishes are made part of the decoration on open shelves.*

Left *Baskets offer attractive and useful storage, particularly for garden produce that needs an air flow to keep fresh, or in a hall for scarves and gloves.*

Right *An attractive iron coat-and-hat stand makes a beguiling, sculptural piece, and replaces a closet.*

Below *This large Shaker box might hold any manner of disparate but untidy essentials, from sewing materials to telephone directories.*

have central heating) and make a room feel cozy; unlined curtains in gauze or colored voile create a casual atmosphere in summer, and fend off inquisitive flies and insects.

Cleaning tasks will seem more agreeable if your utility area, even if it is simply a kitchen corner, has a country feel. Hang brushes and brooms on hooks, and rags along a rack. Cover the ironing board with a pleasing piece of material and expose it folded against the wall. Bring in galvanized iron and zinc rather than plastic buckets and cans. Replace garish plastic brooms, mops, and brushes with wood and bristle ones—just as efficient— and try soft yellow dustcloths and chunks of olive oil soap.

The informality of a country approach can be reflected in everyday storage: wooden egg boxes, old glass cookie jars, or enamel tins. We may not have grown up with the goods and chattels of bygone eras, but the sight of these common objects is comforting, forestalling a more clinically rigid way of living.

Opposite The old-fashioned rocking horse draws the eye down a flagstone corridor into the heart of the home. Household activities are happily exposed in the neat lines of boots and shoes and rows of casual coats. Visitors to this English country house, moving through the passage, are immediately caught up in the mood of easy relaxation that has been created by the family.

Left and below The handsome fish steamer sitting above the door, the terracotta pots of geraniums, waders, and short patterned curtains are intrinsically charming and combine to make an unpretentious, relaxing impression. Elements such as these, and the rustic box with fresh towels (below), have as much to do with establishing a comfortable country style as fine pieces of Limoges would in suggesting elegance.

Above An old long-spouted galvanized watering can goes well with a collection of terracotta pots, and in a city space it will foster the relaxed country mood.

Left The informality of this country kitchen is readily translated to a city space. At its heart is the calm acknowledgment and exposure of every element of kitchen activity, from the creative cooking to the practical dishwashing.

Opposite above and below In keeping with the free and easy open look, the only closed cupboards appear below the work surface. Even the storage containers are made of glass to reveal their contents.

natural materials

This page The items in this display may appear haphazard. But the combination of country objects in various natural materials has been carefully chosen to establish the casually comfortable look of this entrance hall. It is the deliberately symmetrical positioning of the two urns that brings order to what otherwise might look chaotic.

Opposite Such is the freedom to mix and match in comfortable country style that outdoor furniture can find a place indoors. An elegant day bed can be covered with straw-stuffed pillows in almost crude materials, and, in an adventurous move that pays off, wallpaper is torn back to expose the texture of the plaster beneath.

Nature's elements, such as wood, stone, rushes, and grasses, are familiar decorative materials that strike an instinctive chord. The appeal of wooden boxes, stone objects, baskets, and carved bowls is immediate. We want to reach out and touch them. Natural materials make beautiful coverings for floors and furniture; reflecting nature is the aim.

Simple textiles—Aegean stripes, Egyptian cottons, checks—fit this look. Make curtains and covers from unfussy linen scrim, muslin, voile, and burlap (wash before using, as these fabrics tend to shrink). Patterned cottons with botanical prints and stylized flowers make stunning contrasts with these. Simple sprigs, rosebuds, and small blooms with a cottage feel are comfortable country florals.

Walls, too, reflect nature's softer palette: apply paint in duck-egg blue, dawn blush, pale moss green, or the gray and sand of pebbles. Rag rub the paint on or colorwash with several thin coats, for a lightly uneven finish that will reflect the light.

In rooms with these backgrounds of almost chalky tones, place pieces that continue the naturally flat finish. Furniture with a reflective sheen, such as ornately carved mahogany, will not work as effectively in conveying the country feel as unvarnished or traditional painted pieces executed in flat or satin paint. Windsor chairs and wheelbacks have such a familiar link with rural settings that they sit well in comfortable country rooms. Rush or cane chairs are clearly casual. If you find any with sagging seats, tighten them by saturating the seats on both sides with water, then letting them dry naturally.

Scandinavian country-style settles and armchairs, with their curving painted wood frames, look perfectly at home when their upholstery is kept simple. Gingham, stripes, or a small floral print on a white background are striking. Button-backed chairs

convey a relaxed feel when they are covered with heavy-weave undyed parchment cotton or a tea-stained floral fabric. Large, overstuffed sofas and armchairs in slipcovers are far more suggestive of comfortable country than when they are upholstered in formal fabric. Recycle old knitwear as patchwork throws, or pillow covers fastened with bone or wood buttons: particularly effective with original sweaters in natural colors.

Contemporary rugs often have a very uniform pile or a strident pattern. Here is where rag rugs, hook rugs, or the traditional wide woolen weaves of Welsh and New England runners and rugs come into their own. Kelims and oriental rugs are timeless. In sunny rooms, colorful Greek rugs look terrific, particularly as they begin to fade with washing. Sisal and seagrass, patently natural materials, look as good as wall-to-wall covering as they do

Above and opposite In a room decorated in a saturated color, limit the disparate objects in a collection to one shade—the same as the walls or furnishings, or one in striking contrast—or the eye won't know where to settle. In rooms of pallid, natural shades, keep them to a similar palette. The result won't be rustic or primitive, but it will reinforce a sense of peace. Here, a collection of carved stone pieces, fossils, and antlers brings timeless elegance to a sophisticated monochrome city setting. Part of what makes this room so striking is that there is no quarter given to the softening effect of material—no curtains, rugs, or cushions. Fluidity is expressed only in the sculptural lines of the objects on display.

Right Architectural salvage warehouses are inspiring sources for items in natural materials that can make a dramatic impact. The column appears to have been chosen for its fluting, matching that in the leg of the Louis XVI chest beside which it stands.

Below *The house in these pictures is striking for the way in which the decoration sticks firmly to a palette of blues drawn from this color chart, which is used for the dyeing of fabrics and appealing enough to display.*

Opposite *The Gustavian clock in the living room is the starting point for a Scandinavian mood contrived through a collection of simple country pieces in blues and pale grays. The unassuming one-drawer chest fits in well with the raw table and informally upholstered sofa. These things have a lived-in look that suggests a room where shoes can be kicked off and feet rested on the table, yet one that is thoroughly stylish.*

Right *Blue shutters and a blue pillow on the rustic rocking chair leave no room for doubt as to what the owner's favorite color is.*

in an island rug. Hard wearing, and very effective even in a formal setting, they come in simple or complex weaves, some with colors introduced. Terracotta tiles don't have to be limited to kitchen use. Like flagstones, they make handsome flooring and an elegant background for any rug.

Painting floorboards is a striking, economical way to cover the floor that increases the light and, when they are the same color as the walls or woodwork, they give an impression of greater size. Add several coats of varnish to stop the paint from scratching.

Opposite A handsome table and seating formed from stone slabs make the perfect spot on the shaded terrace of a stone house. Cushions in blue provide comfort, as well as softening what might otherwise appear a rather austere spot. The use of the flowerpot as shade for a light adds a witty touch in keeping with the decision to make use of natural materials for this attractive corner.

Left Exposed bricks in the windowseat inside this house offer a rustic touch that is once again tempered by the cushions and curtains in simple fabrics. Their warm blues are echoed in the color of the china pieces displayed on the hutch.

Below A wooden crate, like this one painted a shade of Colonial blue and sitting on a Windsor chair, makes a clever yet unpretentious container for pots of plants and flowers.

Once you have decorated a room, underline the feel with details. Here is where you can have fun. Stone garden urns, spotted with lichen, make a stunning impact on an indoor table or mantel. A pretty Victorian birdcage, set where the light from a window can travel through its delicate bars; seashells along a mantel; terra-cotta flowerpots filled with plants—all carry the theme of pastoral idyll. Newspapers can be tossed into a wooden basket or stenciled crate by an armchair, while glass garden bells and lobster pots can double as shades for hanging lights. Light shining through these graphic shapes is dramatic, but use low-watt bulbs or they will dazzle, and anchor fixtures securely.

Elements like these remind us of the pleasure we derive from the integrity of natural materials and living with things shaped by human hands from nature's bounty.

Left *Why not demonstrate an appreciation of wood, the warmest and most generous of natural materials? Here, picturesque, paint-peeling folding chairs are stored propped open in this shelter off the patio, giving the wry impression that this area should be celebrated by people taking the time to sit and admire it. They add a decorative touch that makes a set piece out of a practical storage place.*

Above *Old beams are too often painted over. Exposed, they add a glow that justifies the effort required to strip them. But it is a laborious process. Sand-blasting leaves a film of dust over every surface in the house for a considerable time after the job is completed. Nonetheless, it is probably a safer option than applying chemical stripper—only practical when undertaken with extreme care in a space that is well ventilated.*

country
rooms

COUNTRY living rooms

A welcoming sofa, a vase of flowers, and a few favorite pieces. With simple but well-chosen ingredients you can create a living room that is a place of perfect comfort.

Comfortable country style lends itself to an easeful look. This need not imply that you will veer toward inelegance. Any room that is uncomplicated will be a relaxing one to sit in. Easy on the eye, it shouldn't contain too many elements fighting for attention. Armchairs should look inviting, enticing you to curl up in them with a good book. A side table within reach to support a lamp or a bowl of flowers confirms the feel.

In your living room, begin by considering what you want its focal point to be. It might be the view through a window, a wall on which you hang a favorite painting, or a fireplace. Next, decide seating and where you plan to place it. Your most important furniture decision will be the sofa. You may choose not to have one—groups of cozy armchairs look very congenial. Two sofas can be set with a low table between them, or placed in an L-shape. Big sofas with a sociable saggy appearance, in untailored linen slipcovers, piled with throws and cushions to sink into, are seductive. However, a sofa that's a little more structured is just as appropriate when the informality is conveyed

your living room is a reflection
of your private self—
to truly relax and be comfortable here, you have
to be yourself

Above and right *This modest country house brims with its owner's personality. Distinctly feminine, it has been decorated with an unexpected sumptuousness that never becomes too fussy. Extravagantly sized cushions slump over the stone staircase leading down from the hall and along the built-in seating beside the fire; tables are covered with thick capacious cloths; and swathes of lightweight materials are draped dramatically around the windows. Yet by keeping white as the predominant color, none of this opulence is too much, and an easy elegance prevails in this fundamentally plain cottage.*

by its upholstery—a wide stripe in cotton-candy pink, or bold blue and white checks. These aren't earnest fabrics. They sing with country freshness. Or take a sofa with graphic lines. Lay a length of cloth along the seat or across the back, and immediately you deflate its solemnity. Even the formality of a more decorative Gustavian sofa can be tempered by pale painted walls and furniture to imbue the living room with tranquility.

Any living room is rendered simple by keeping every major piece in it in one color. This can be very effective when that color is white. Splashes of a different shade can be added in cushions, sofa throws, an embroidered or tapestry rug, or with bowls of flowers.

Left and opposite White establishes a mood that is totally relaxing. This room is modest in size, with tiled stairs in one corner leading upstairs. By adhering to white in its decoration and keeping it uncluttered, the space feels generous and restful. Furniture and ornaments are simple. Even the floor is rug free, increasing the feeling of space.

Below Again, white forms the background to a room that is invitingly comfortable. The armchair looks invitingly cozy, thanks to its gathered skirt, while the use of color on its cushions and on the covers of those pillows in the alcove lounging area draws the eye to them and encourages an awareness that these are places in which to relax thoroughly.

This page *Informal seating can be the key to creating a relaxing atmosphere. In this room, the windowseat is an inviting place for friends to sit. Intimacy is conveyed by the feminine colors and the lace at the window.*

Opposite *The built-in sofa in this barnlike summer poolhouse is a tranquil spot offering comfort among its generous abundance of cushions and pillows.*

Color is crucial in setting the tone. For example, in a confidently elegant living room containing treasures in elemental wood, stone, bone, and glass, keep the background to a single color—say, a spectrum of whites. At the other end of the scale, jewel colors like sapphire, amethyst, or emerald inspire contentment, by bringing in the vibrant tones we associate with warmth and sunshine.

Classic patterns and materials, used in an unconventional manner, shy away from formality. In a room decorated in a striking *toile de Jouy*, using the upholstery design on the walls makes for a far-from-conservative outcome. A sofa in front of a large window may have a traditionally tailored cover. But placing a patio-style wooden chair and a garden bench in front of it, and having florals as the sofa material to echo the greenery outside, makes the setting relaxed.

Keep window treatments simple. Unadorned poles with gathered curtains in plain or uncomplicated materials and patterns work best. Unwelcome views can be disguised with plain muslin or voile.

How you introduce light is important. Candelabras and chandeliers have wonderful flowing lines. But err on the side of restraint in design. Anything too ornate will look out of place. Candles can be put to use on mantels or in clusters in the fireplace. Mirrors double any light

Opposite *Windows are wonderful places to sit beside. This sumptuous couch oozes comfort and calls out for someone to relax on it. The mix of prints, which reflects the garden beyond the striking single pane, is soothing because it is restricted to soft tones.*

Below *Here, too, the variety of different patterns and materials used for the pillows has an inviting appeal.*

and enlarge space. Old ones in unpainted pine frames or French *faux* bamboo, their backs a little bitten, have immense charm.

Table lamps with gingham, floral, or Colonial-style cut-parchment-work shades make a comfortable country statement. The pools of light from lamps are far more intimate and informal than the fiercer glare from one central fixture. Country farmhouse finds, like lidded enamel churns, thick glass cider jars, or pottery crocks can be converted into appealing lamp bases. Ceramic or wooden bases in simple cylindrical or rectangular

shapes are effective. Wall sconces made from metal, or even plaster or tile meant for outdoors, have a guileless feel.

Fresh flowers bring a room to life. Anything home grown will encourage a comfortable country feel: mixed flowers in a pretty pitcher, or large terra-cotta pots of daisies set on the floor look effortlessly relaxed. Old-fashioned roses strike a timeless note. During fall and winter, display bowls of dried lavender or rose-petal potpourri to add a seasonal touch and scent. A basket of pinecones ready to throw on the fire will have the same effect.

Opposite left *Not only does the striking antique mirror increase light and the sense of space, but it makes its own decorative statement. The patterned candlesticks on the white Gustavian desk add an appealing sculptural interest and draw attention to the mirror.*

Opposite right *Deliberately chosen details will add focus to a room. Individual flowers in a collection of glass bottles make a charmingly casual display that softens an imposing formal mantelpiece. It's an idea that puts a collection of pretty perfume bottles and decanters to effective use.*

Right *Draping a throw and assorted pillows over the singularly elegant sofa in a period city house relaxes its contemporary lines. Informality is introduced to this urban setting through the eclectic yet careful choice of country pieces that are united by a white paint finish.*

Below *On the pretty Gustavian settle, the rectangular pillow draws the eye to its appealing shape.*

fresh flowers bring a room to life:
handpicked blooms in
a collection of favorite glass bottles and vases
look effortless

candlesticks in cut glass
or silver set on side tables close to a window
reflect daylight

Left and below left *A scalloped border makes the cover of this armchair as unceremonious as a summer skirt. The shape of this original touch is echoed in the glass chandelier used as table decoration. So close to the window, its cut-glass pendants trap the sunlight.*

Below *The white china cabinet is positioned where it will absorb and reflect the light coming in from outside.*

Opposite *This informal, light-filled living room has a wonderfully nostalgic feel. Folds of fine voile at the windows, a sofa throw of lace, the crocheted mat beneath the bowl of roses, and a wicker veranda chair are all suggestive of a tea party attended by women in veiled hats—and all contribute to the atmosphere. The old-fashioned bed tray has been given a new lease on life, serving as a witty coffee table.*

COUNTRY kitchens

A pot of basil set near the stove, ivory china on a cream-painted hutch—comfort and tranquility in the kitchen and dining room are conveyed by simple touches like these.

Cooking and eating can be relaxing occupations, and should be enjoyed in comfortable surroundings. Culinary fashion no longer requires sauces to be reduced to within a splash of their lives; this also takes the pressure off the way our kitchens and dining rooms look.

Where and how you cook and eat depends primarily on how much space you have. If your dining room is separate from your kitchen, consider it as another living room. Do you want space for sitting away from the table before or after the meal, on a sofa or in a windowseat? Is there a working fireplace in the room and enough space for a table in front of it that the backs of diners won't burn? And what sort of table do you plan to install? A table designed specifically for a dining room is likely to be more formal than the average kitchen table. Your choice of table is especially key if you expect to eat in the kitchen. Here, the table you eat at is likely to do double duty as a work surface. A scrubbed pine table or a plank tabletop on a pair of trestles sets an immediately accommodating tone.

If you then install freestanding pieces of furniture instead of built-in systems, you create an even more informal setting. Shelved cupboards and armoires for china and glass are good-looking repositories with a country feel; chests of drawers make storage just as efficient for pots and pans as kitchen cabinets do. It may be that a galley arrangement is the

Opposite A hutch has been created out of wall shelves hung above a wood-topped sideboard. While it provides storage for the household's dinnerware, its practicality has not been allowed to override its visual appeal. The display of plates is carefully arranged.

This page Honeyed wood on cabinet doors, table, and chairs makes a kitchen-dining room congenially informal. Kitchen equipment, herbs, and utensils are hung on hooks in a decorative touch that effectively reinforces the relaxed spirit of the room.

This page Some things strike an immediate chord of comfort and serenity: a generous kitchen range, a cozy blanket loosely covering a chair, and the tools for food preparation and eating happily on display.

Opposite above The kitchen is one public room that people are seldom dismayed to find in a state of industrious disarray. Cupboards and shelves filled with dishes and cooks' ingredients make a beguiling display, like this one with its charming period dinnerware and packaging.

Opposite below A carefully arranged sideboard presentation of pretty bowls is a comforting sight.

a farmhouse range

draws people to its warm generosity in

country or city

most practical in your space. In this case, think about installing a prefabricated counter unit carcass, but hanging your own pine doors or pretty curtains. The same approach works with shelving built from brick or wood.

Pots and pans can be brought out on show, with oven gloves and herbs, hung from hooks or rods within easy reach of the stove. Having the necessary tools and equipment at hand makes cooking as relaxing to perform as to watch. Spoons and spatulas can be plunged into an old pitcher; lids and chopping boards kept in wire baskets; potted herbs ranged along a windowsill. If it looks casual, everyone will feel casual.

The stove, too, is a serious issue. A large farmhouse range establishes a sense of comfort and ease, drawing people and pets to hang around its ample generosity. But a similar response can be inspired by a more casual cooking arrangement: a below-counter wall oven with burners above, set into a tiled surround, for example. A sense of informality is best conveyed by keeping larger appliances below counter level, rather than the more conventional urban look of double ovens installed at shoulder height. A freestanding refrigerator is more likely to give a city kitchen a comfortable country feel than a built-in appliance.

Sinks can also set the tone. Large ceramic sinks are generally deeper than stainless-steel sinks and consequently far more practical. French farmhouse-style sinks, also ceramic, are shallow but usually much wider. The extra space of both makes washing leafy vegetables or handling fish easier.

This page and opposite Incorporating a dining area into the kitchen can be an open-plan success, as these pictures show. The kitchen need not impose its own character on the whole space. Here a dining area with its own atmosphere and style has been created within a large country kitchen. A 1930s-style table provides generous dining space beneath an elaborate chandelier and is surrounded by ocher garden chairs. This dining zone is demarcated by the old Spanish rug upon which the table sits, and the presence of a wicker chaise longue and armchair by the French doors in which to relax. Equally, the cooking area is defined by a breakfast table set at an angle, parallel to the range, under a billiard light that points up the different use of this area.

This page and opposite Here a dining table is tucked into the cozy corner of an entrance hall. The built-in seating area beside the imposing fireplace, with its piles of over-sized pillows, sets a carefree tone of luxury and relaxation that is accentuated by the looped voile swag. Using printed fabric for the pillows and tablecloth keeps the look casual and comfortable.

Companies selling professional catering equipment can put you in touch with manufacturers who will design stainless-steel sinks to any depth or width you desire, with integrated, seamless draining boards and preparation areas on either side that are a boon to the serious cook. Lined up next to a wooden surfaced or marble-topped table or drawered chest, their industrial appearance is toned down. You can also have sinks and work surfaces made from concrete in a natural or a stained color (be careful not to put glass or china down too quickly, or it will shatter). You may need to reinforce any floor that is not at ground level, to take the extra weight.

Old brass faucets look wonderfully rustic, but make sure that flea-market finds have a thread compatible with your plumbing system. Faucets bought in Europe, for instance, often won't fit in the United States. Hospital faucets, with their long handles running parallel to the back of the sink, are immensely practical for turning on and off with elbows when you are busy cooking. Should you prefer not to have a splashback—though marble, stone, and plain or patterned tiles all promote a comfortable country look—make sure you paint the wall behind the sink or stove with acrylic or gloss paint so you can wipe the wall down and keep it from staining.

Before you decide on lighting, consider how and where you work. Lighting should

take a length of gingham
or a floral sheet as tablecloth, or large napkins to suggest
a generous host

be placed so you do not cast a shadow over your preparation area. Similarly, will you want to shed several pools of light over your dining table, or just one, or will the place where you eat be illuminated from the walls with the table softly candlelit? You don't want anything so modern that it looks out of place, but you do want it to be effective. Opaque glass shades look immensely appealing on hanging lamps and, along with enamel or metal saucer-shaped shades, can still be picked up in flea markets and thrift stores.

If you are planning on a single kitchen-dining room and it is a room large enough to keep the two elements well apart, you can visually separate the dining area by running the lighting on a two-circuit system so that both ends of the room are not necessarily lit at once. A dimmer on the dining-end circuit is also a good idea. If it is a small room with space for only a little table, try turning it into a stylish kitchen-dining room with a very French, almost boudoir feel. Hang a pretty but unexpected glass chandelier above a curvaceous set of iron café chairs and table, and paint the room in pale pastel colors.

Different lamps or lampshades establish the two separate areas further, as will a change in flooring. You might, at the working end of the room, have an easy-to-clean tiled or stone floor and, at the dining end, wooden floorboards, parquet, or a large rug. In a city kitchen that is not at ground

Opposite This dining room mixes different patterns, but in similar hues. The checks on the covers of the folding chairs echo the green of the curtains behind the glass cabinet doors. The quilted tablecloth borrows from a classic Victorian fashion.

Above left Shades of blue play a strong role in the decoration of this kitchen, with blue patterned wallpaper, the pretty hutch door frames highlighted in a strong shade, and a blue and white edging lining the shelves.

Above right Blue continues in the tiles and pitchers around the marble sink.

This picture and right This is a wonderfully whimsical kitchen, as relaxing as it is welcoming. Shelves above a wall lined in rough wooden boards are edged with ruffles, and cushions sag over the edges of the chairs at the Moroccan dining table. Seashells have been pressed into the curvaceous concrete splashback behind the circular sink. An intricate chandelier adds a romantic flourish.

bring the country inside:
abundant pots of greenery suggest a conservatory
dining room

Right *The imposing cast-iron fireplace, with its display of handsome pewter platters along the mantelshelf, draws the eye in this simple but comfortable country dining room. Its austere lines are softened by the pottery display. Any style of furniture other than the absolutely plain pine table and kitchen chairs would risk seeming excessive against it. Restraint continues in the style of the simple lampshade and the curtains hung on a plain metal pole.*

Left *A pleasing country-style cushion for this handsome Windsor chair has been sewn out of cotton dishcloths.*

level, be sure to find out how much weight the ceiling of the room below can take before you go ahead with stone flooring.

Once you have organized the main pieces, bring in accessories that will confirm the look. In the kitchen, classic ironware, enamelware, and terra-cotta cooking equipment is as handsome and efficient today as it ever was. Similarly, pottery, glassware, and china can be as casual and diverse as you please. Almost any pottery—plain, patterned, or colored—can be set out successfully alongside wooden bowls, metal platters, and bone spoons. One-off handmade pieces have a particular charm, but simple mass-produced shapes in sunshine colors, like the Fiestaware of the 1950s, also have a wonderful appeal. Patterned dinner sets in soft berry or moss colors on an ivory background still convey a comfortable country feel without being quite so rudimentary in style. Plain cream china on a plain cream-painted hutch looks as effective in a kitchen or dining room as a glass-fronted cabinet filled with a disparate collection of pretty pieces of pottery in blues. Equally, setting a table with mismatched plates and bistro-style glasses can be as warmly welcoming as the more formal array of a Provençal dinner set on a scrubbed pine table. In the absence of old embroidered napkins, use plain or patterned dishcloths; their exuberant size suggests a liberal host.

COUNTRY bedrooms

One room in which you must be able to relax is the bedroom. The easy, serene style of a comfortable country bedroom makes the perfect place for refreshing rest.

The bedroom is the oasis of the house, a place in which we can restore ourselves away from public view. Everything in it should invite relaxation, beginning with the bed. A comfortable country room is not the place for a sharp cosmopolitan design. A bed to establish the mood could be anything from a brass or a painted iron frame to a wooden sleigh bed or a four-poster. But if yours is just a mattress on a bed base, a more mellow look is easily achieved by hanging a quilt, pretty piece of fabric, screen, or carved wooden panel behind it to create an informal headboard.

Soften the bed itself with layers of inviting linen, blankets, and pillows. A tailored cover could look too restrained here. A quilt, a length of charming material, or a lace or cotton-crocheted top, turned back to expose sheets and pillows, will look far more appealing. Any

Above Yellow curtains add a cheerful splash of color to this white-painted child's bedroom with its iron crib and miniature table set for tea with teddy.

Left This comfortable haven in light-blue painted boards was designed by a grandmother to provide a special bed for her grandchild.

Opposite right Quilts, bed linen, and pillows of different patterned blues are layered to striking effect, giving this bedroom, with its painted iron bedsteads and fantasy voile canopies hanging from a painted border and blue valance, a peaceful aspect.

Opposite left An appliquéd cushion adds a personal touch to a comfortable country white wicker chair.

Opposite *This distinctive bedroom is thoroughly stylish yet supremely comfortable. Soothing soft green walls have been dramatically stenciled; vintage bed linen covers the antique iron bed under its striped canopy.*

Left *Another, more formal canopy, combined with sprigged wallpaper and lace at the window, makes a romantic sanctuary of a girl's bedroom.*

Far left *Even the robe hanging on the back of the door has a design contribution to make.*

Below *The unusually patterned and painted iron bed is just one contributor to the great character of this room.*

old-fashioned bedding will look perfect here: eiderdowns, comforters, wool or cotton blankets folded at the end of the bed, or bolsters will all suggest a tempting refuge from the world. Pillows don't have to be slipped into matching covers. A mix of plain cotton with lace-trimmed or embroidered pillowcases is stunning. To finish, pile on pillows in different patterns and fabrics—but in one or two colors only, to keep the look serene.

Bed linen in white looks appealingly pure and fresh, but striped or checked sheets also have the clean, crisp aspect you should strive for. Keep them the same color in which you have decorated the rest of the room, or the simplicity is lost.

If your ceiling is high enough, you can have fun above the bed draping canopies in muslin, voile, or net, by threading the material romantically through a rounded door knocker, or installing a tiara-shaped frame against the wall from which to drape fabric. Put short rods at head height on each side of the pillows from which to hang pretty lace panels, and gain privacy and tranquility.

Beds are conventionally set against a wall, but this needn't be a hard and fast rule. Consider placing the bed lengthwise along a window to catch a view, or against the back of a freestanding armoire that becomes a screen between the bed and the door.

A surface close to the pillow on which to lay down a book is useful. It doesn't have to be a table; a painted linen chest or a simple wooden chair is an informal touch. A plainly upholstered buttonback chair doubles as a place to read when you don't want to relax on the bed. If there is space for somewhere to sit—a small sofa at the end of the bed, a modest armchair by a fireplace or window—the room becomes a haven you will enjoy at any time of day, particularly if it contains some of your favorite treasures.

Unless there is a view you would prefer to obscure—in which case a simple shade in a plain material should do the trick—keep the decoration of your windows as unfussy as you can. Narrow lengths of fabric on each side of the window will soften the more metropolitan look of a shade on its own. Curtains should be as plain as possible; one color in cotton, voile, or muslin. If you prefer

a rug by the bed
to land warm toes on each morning
is comforting

This page and opposite *A simple bedroom with a comfortable country feel can be achieved with a little planning and thought. Here, the French bed has been deliberately set across the window and is dressed almost entirely in blue, proving that blues don't always have to match. Only the bottom sheet, a white embroidered pillowcase glimpsed between a solid and a checked blue pillow, and the blue and white check of the folded blanket provide a break. The room's austerity is toned down by the charming heirloom dollhouse set on an old painted box, and the old rag rug by the bed.*

a patterned fabric, pick a small design. Curtains made from antique sheets or tablecloths can look inspired. Sprigged florals are pretty; checks, stripes, and ticking offer less feminine alternatives. Hang curtains from a simple wooden or iron pole, with wooden or brass rings, or tabs or ties made from the fabric.

A freestanding armoire can convey the kind of informality you are striving for better than built-in closets, although you can soften these with a decorative trim or by cutting shapes in their doors. If a mounted clothes rod is your only option, think about exposing your clothes on wooden hangers or stuffed hangers covered in pretty fabrics, especially if you tend to buy clothes in the same color palette. Shelves of neatly folded piles of sweaters in similar tones look wonderfully restful. If you don't think you can keep your clothing neat enough for public view, run a casual curtain above the rod. The natural texture of burlap or linen scrim looks very effective used this way. The rod itself could even be made of a length of driftwood.

Opposite top *Here voile softens strong checks that have been mixed with an Edwardian quilt for striking impact on a white-painted French Directoire bed.*

Opposite bottom right *A carved Asian screen, behind the bed, dominates a room whose unusual length allows for a bathtub (behind the screen on the left).*

This page *An iron bed placed under the eaves and hung with voile becomes a romantic space and makes full use of a room with a sloping roof, minimizing its awkwardness. The painted dresser echoes the reds in the quilt.*

Opposite bottom left *Embroidered pillows have a timeless charm.*

Below The eye is drawn to this invitingly comfortable armchair by the matching pink dado that runs round the wall. The reading light confirms the intention that this corner can be used for relaxation at any time.

Right Pink is a soothing color, as these pillows, in toile de Jouy edged with pink ticking, and the soft quilt beneath them demonstrate.

Opposite A bedroom that is merely a place in which to sleep is a waste of valuable space. This should be a room so comfortable and alluring you will be drawn to spending restorative time in it during the day. Here a curvaceous rocking chair and pretty French country chair, in front of an inviting fireplace, have been chosen to encourage the bedroom's owner to use it as a room in which to sit and read.

Strictly speaking, comfortable country bedroom floors should be bare, covered only in rugs. For extra cosseting in the winter months, overlap different rugs all over the floor, editing them back once the weather improves. If you prefer carpet, consider seagrass or sisal or a flat wool weave in a natural tone.

Painted floorboards make a room look bigger and lighter. The color you choose for your walls will also have an influence: dark shades will not only make the room shrink, but they won't be in keeping with the overall style. Focus on whites—remembering that white itself comes in a range of tones from soft to bright—and pales, or tints of pastels like lavender, fern, or rose. Shades of blue give a stronger, more masculine look, if you choose those reflecting the warm azures of the Mediterranean, the colors in Moorish tiles, or hues of Provençal pots.

somewhere to sit
makes your bedroom a restorative
haven

COUNTRY bathrooms

In this room devoted to pampering, gather your favorite things—fine soaps, scents, and sumptuous towels—and relax while you wash away the cares of the day.

in the bathroom
indulge your senses and promote
wellbeing

Opposite and below *This charming room has a Victorian clawfoot tub with Victorian flowered tiles, repeated over the* toile de Jouy-*curtained marble basin (below), where they make an attractive splashback. Pretty Limoges and other plates, the paintings, the French mirror and wall lights above the basin, and the wicker conservatory chair have all been chosen for their Victorian feel.*

Left *Here the same look is given a more masculine interpretation. The mirror above the Edwardian basin is simply framed, and the splashback of English Victorian tiles, restricted to blues, looks less feminine. Tiles like these can be found in antique stores, but plain ones work as well. Both rooms may have an agreeably relaxed feel, but their decoration has been carefully planned.*

Having a bath is a superbly comfortable way of slowing down. Bathing is not simply to do with getting clean; a shower can do that. The ritual of running the water, adding a swoosh of scented salts or a glug of luxurious oil, then sliding down for a long soak, makes having a bath a ceremony. Only if your shower is outdoors, and you can scrub under a warm sun or with the twinkle of stars overhead, can the experience of showering be as sensual.

Rolltop or clawfoot bathtubs set in the middle of the room project a restful look, by suggesting there is no need to make maximum, practical, use of the space. These old-fashioned tubs, now copied by modern manufacturers, recall the days when a bathroom looked like another living room, with a fire in the grate and a sofa or day bed on which to recline. It's an atmosphere you can easily emulate, just by bringing an armchair into the room.

In smaller rooms, set the bathtub under a window with a pleasant view, or up against a wall. A tub on feet—and basin on a pedestal—will make a small room look airier because the eye can

This page One of the critical issues in bathroom design is where to store clutter. Bathrooms are home to quantities of bottles, brushes, and bathing equipment, which if all on view can make the room appear chaotic and an unwelcoming mess. In this bathroom, with the handsome look of its Victorian mahogany-surround tub softened by lace curtains at the window, all but the most attractive bottles are stored away.

Opposite This thoughtful display of bathroom equipment is appealing because each article, made from natural materials, is designed without ostentation. There are no garish accessories or oddly fashioned soaps. These glass bottles, printed boxes, and cotton towels are plain and unpretentious, yet attractive.

travel beyond them to the wall and floor behind. Faucets that come with a "telephone" shower attachment are extremely useful for hair washing and informal showering. If you want a real shower against the wall, pick one with a very large head for a generous downpour. Hang two shower curtains, pinning each one on alternate curtain rings— something waterproof or quick drying for inside the rim, with a pretty curtain to disguise it hanging down on the outside.

A wall or sill against which a bathtub is pushed will need protection from splashes. A wooden windowsill is a convenient place to keep lotions and oils, or even a book, but try not to drip over it when reaching for what you need. Several coats of gloss paint will prevent the wood from becoming damp. A wall might need a splashback of tiles; several rows of antique tiles produce a country feel.

A narrow bathroom, carved from a convenient corner of the house, can still be a place of comfort. With room only for a built-in bathtub, convey a sense of spaciousness by keeping the decoration of the room in one soft shade or white, and add touches of color through details like towels.

If the room is too small for any but a drop-in basin, consider, with the help of a good plumber, installing the basin in the carefully cut-out top of an old chest of drawers, rather than having a manufactured bathroom cabinet. The bowl will take up the first drawer, but the others will provide plenty of room for toiletries, towels, or medicines, and the look of the piece will add a comfortable country touch. If there isn't room for such a large item, an antique washstand can be put to work at its original job, housing your bottles and brushes, with towels or magazines stacked on the lower ledge.

abundant thick towels
and bowls of fine soaps are
luxurious

This page *This bathroom has been pared down to a simple combination of pale floorboards, ivory-painted tongue-and-groove walls, and a door that draws attention to both the beautiful wooden beams around the room and the old cast-iron bathtub and basin, elegantly painted rich charcoal. In a clever idea borrowed from the kitchen, hooks run along the towel rod to hold the smaller towels and washcloths.*

Right *A simple wooden chair draws attention to the fact that, while the wooden door has been painted, the plank wall is bare.*

Bookshelves are also a storage alternative. Pretty painted ironwork stands with glass shelves look light and airy. Don't limit yourself to filling them with bathing paraphernalia. Why not display some of your favorite china or bowls? Chairs are useful in bathrooms, to lay clothes or towels upon, as the means of introducing a pattern or color on a cushion or upholstery, and of course to sit on. You could also hang pictures or photographs, as long as the room is well ventilated—built-up steam will damage your pictures as the dampness inevitably seeps behind the glass.

Elsewhere in the house, comfortable country style tends toward simplicity, but in the bathroom luxury and comfort mean abundance. Give in to the desire to pamper yourself by bringing in big natural sponges, wood and natural-bristle nailbrushes and backscrubs, and old-fashioned china colander soap dishes to hold the current bar of scented soap.

Choose bathmats and towels of a generous size. Stick to a soft palette if you want any color other than plain white—pale pinks, blues, grays, taupes, or lavender. Striped towels look fresh and pretty, especially interspersed with others in a single tone. A linen bag dangling behind the door or attractive bathrobes hung on a row of hooks along a wall are casually decorative possibilities.

Exploit a natural light source with a beautiful panel or curtain of lace, or a length of patterned sheer, to give privacy without blocking the daylight. Good lighting makes a bathroom look bigger and more inviting. Run it off a two-circuit system: lights over mirrors should be strong enough to be useful, and having softer lighting in the ceiling above the tub or around the walls means you can change the mood to fit your own. All you need is time to enjoy it.

Above The beach pebbles and toy boat on the ledge of this bathroom window recall the sea and the pleasures of the beach, establishing a relaxed mood. Bowls of shells or pieces of driftwood used as rods for curtains, hooks for robes, or simply as sculptural shapes all look pleasing in a bathroom. A dishcloth hung on clips is an amusing curtain.

Opposite This compact bathroom has enormous personality. Fragments of mirror and glass pressed into the wall make a light-reflecting mosaic. Much is made of the power of reflection, in the number of mirrors in the tiny space, and in the unusual informal dado of zinc that runs below the rough shelf.

COUNTRY outdoors

An outside space, large or small, offers a sense of renewal. A bench beneath a tree, a row of plants along a windowsill—anything that links us to nature adds an air of ease.

Left *Don't forget to make time to sit in your glorious garden and savor the results of all your hard work. Choose where and what you sit on carefully so you make the most of the view. Arbors and bowers create thoroughly romantic settings. Here, prettily sinuous chairs and table are set out for tea under a heady shower of roses.*

Opposite top *This curved bench is painted pale gray, a gentler contrast to the vivid dark pink roses forming an arch over it than the more usual white.*

Opposite left *A beautifully ornate white-painted wire chair holds its own against an exuberant rose bush, its lines echoing those of the nearby pedestal.*

Opposite right *An overhanging canopy of wisteria and a flight of outdoor steps sporting terra-cotta pots of plants and herbs frame this quiet corner—an ideal place to sit on a mat-covered ledge of stones at a rustic stone table.*

Eating outdoors, perhaps on a terrace under a vine, conjures up one of the most alluring aspects of comfortable country style. It recalls childhood picnics, romantic dinners under the stars, and long lunches with family and friends.

You don't need a vast country garden to achieve the same atmosphere. A small graveled or paved city patio, terrace, or backyard filled with flowering pots can be just as beguiling a venue. Spread a pretty length of fabric or a faded antique cloth over a table, surround it with mismatched chairs, and cover it with casual china, and you leave the metropolis far behind.

The garden, the terrace, or the backyard are essentially rooms like any other, so you should approach them as such. Decide if you want your outdoor space to be a pretty-parasol, Edwardian-tea-gown place or to have a more market-umbrella, casual-cottons atmosphere. Rattan or woven cane chairs or wooden slatted café chairs with peeling paint look wonderfully indolent outside in the sun. Deckchairs with plain cream canvas or sun-bleached Madras stripes are casually comfortable and, along with canvas-seated directors' chairs, have the

advantage in a small space of being easy to fold and store away. Masses of cushions with covers of stripes and florals, tossed onto rugs on the ground or stone benches against a cool wall, make seating especially inviting on drowsy afternoons.

A day bed or steamer chair covered by a full-length cushion in natural textured cotton makes for real elegance outside. Pretty curling ironwork chairs at a small marble-topped table form an inviting spot for a morning cup of coffee. Wooden benches, either unpainted, rustic, and touched with age and dabs of lichen, or coolly graceful in an undulating shape with a coat of glossy white paint, encourage you to sit and relax any time of day. Set one under a bower of roses, clematis, or wisteria, or between large pots of blooming flowers; once you are seated, there will be little impetus to move.

Unpainted furniture looks more informal than painted, while pieces glossed in white have a fresh appeal that speaks of breezes and boats skidding across sparkling water.

Above *The impressive garden room on these pages may be informal, but great care has gone into its decoration. A bust of Marie Antoinette peeps wittily out through the plants and pots. These objects can be placed elsewhere if the room is needed to entertain guests.*

Left *Three enormous architectural windows allow light and air to flood into the room. With its pale butter-colored walls echoing the sunshine and its high beamed ceiling painted white, the vast space provides a calm and soothing summer sanctuary.*

Opposite *Stuccoes dot the walls, while a mirror hanging above the bench brings a reflection of the garden beyond. Plants, pots, and stones litter the long table and stand about among watering cans on the pale square-stoned floor, an indication of the casual use to which the room is generally put.*

Furniture in the vibrant blues, yellows, and mellow reds of the Mediterranean will bring a feel of the Riviera to any setting.

You can define your own comfortable country atmosphere just by laying the table for a meal outside. A blue and white checked cloth, with bowls and plates in robust colors and rustic shapes, establishes quite a different mood from a table laid with delicate, soft-colored dishes on a pretty damask cloth. The mood will be informal if you forget uniformity and regularity. For a look that is sumptuously generous and casual at the same time, use a plain white sheet as a huge cloth that drops to the ground. Serving bowls in both vibrant glazes and simple terra-cotta, one-off pieces that don't match, a harlequin set of glasses, different napkins—a mix of these will combine to create an atmosphere that encourages people to sit back and enjoy themselves.

A weathered picnic table with benches on each side makes an informal setting for lunch outside. With covered pads or a folded quilt to sit on, you add comfort without spoiling the effect. Decorate the table with a terra-cotta pot of flowers rather than cut blooms and even if it sits on a city patio, you make the garden link.

Fill a terrace or a tiny backyard with as many terra-cotta flowerpots in different shapes and sizes as you have room for. Place pots of herbs closest to the table so that diners can reach

Opposite *Outdoor living is a celebration of summer. When the warm weather comes, we must make the most of it, by enjoying relaxed meals at simple tables outside. This one set under a wisteria bower by blue shutters and a blue-painted kitchen door is given an enticing look with the generous sweep of its plain linen cloth.*

Below *A swing hung from a shady tree is guaranteed to attract children.*

Above left *A platter and a bowl of garden vegetables awaiting the hand of the cook make an attractive display. The table is casual, the cloth a little rumpled, forks collected haphazardly inside a napkin, everything contributing to a comfortably relaxed mood.*

Above right *Plants of contrasting leaf and height crowd this rustic garden table, ready to be planted out or simply left where they are to please the eye.*

Above *Summer tables are fun to decorate. The shape and color of glossy red cherries in a white bowl are echoed in the baubles in the stems of these wine glasses.*

Opposite *A view of the long summer garden seen across the top of the stone garden table laid for brunch. The different shades of blue around and on this summer table contrast attractively with the bright verdant shade of the blooming garden.*

Left *A bird's-eye view of the contrasting patterns of blues. The Mediterranean striped cushions work well with the tablecloth's crisp checks. Smooth cobblestones form a cool, practical terrace floor beneath the garden table. Consider where to put a summer table: if it is set on a lawn, the grass will be scuffed long before the season is over.*

Below *The porch is a tranquil place for the family of the house to gather and relax.*

out to pinch them and release their aromas. Grow highly scented flowers—jasmine, lavender, or a rose—by the door into the house to send the smell of sweetness wafting indoors on a breeze.

Establish a creeper or vine—easy to grow in most mild climates—and quite soon you will have runners to pull over and create a canopy above your table if you choose. It is a good idea, even in a small space, to make some part of your seating area shaded. A canopy attached to a wall that you can reel in and out is one option, a plain umbrella a simpler one. Or keep an umbrella stand full of paper parasols and a basket brimming with sunhats by the back door.

At night, light candles. You can prevent them from blowing out by putting them inside glass, either shapely hurricane shades or the replacement glass shades sold by most department stores for converted Victorian oil lamps. When the night is still, a chandelier filled with candles, hung somewhere where the melting wax won't cause problems, makes a stunning effect.

Opposite The house on these pages demonstrates how much can be achieved in a small space. A pool of modest size and the house behind it are made to look larger and more airy by the stretch of reflective French doors looking from the house to the pool.

Right A rose arbor provides shade and a place to sit and dry off. Against the far wall, under the climbing vine where a towel hangs, is an outdoor shower. The pretty painted iron armchair dates from the 1930s. Country fairs are still good sources for similar pieces.

Below The French doors continue around the house to form the entrance into the kitchen-dining room. Frames on the doors have been painted the soft aquamarine that has also been used on the folding café chairs in the garden. Flower-filled terra-cotta pots in different shapes and sizes have been set out around the base of the walls and along the edge of the terrace to add softness, scent, and color to this serene setting.

You can create a garden room inside with pots of plants and flowers. Set them on the floor or on a garden bench just inside the door to link with the green outside. Hang a mirror to reflect the garden. Keep everything airy; sit on steamer chairs, cane or willow chairs, and floral rugs, and keep any shelving for books or ornaments unobtrusive. Have outdoor things around—a flower basket for papers or a farm stool for a side table. Then, when it is too hot or too cold to sit outside, you will feel refreshed by the sense of almost being in it. Even if an outdoor room means a tiny balcony or a strip of flagstones, make the most of it. Fill it with tubs of flowers and herbs; paint the exterior wall white to increase the light. Pull out the stops for your own comfortable country corner in the sun.

SOURCE DIRECTORY

UNITED STATES
Antiques and Decoration

ABC CARPET & HOME
888 Broadway
New York
NY 10003
212 473 3000

BARDITH LTD ANTIQUES
901 Madison Avenue
New York
NY 10021
212 737 3775

BARNEYS
660 Madison Avenue
New York
NY 10021
212 826 8900

BRIDGE KITCHENWARE
214 E 52nd Street
New York
NY 10022
1 800 274 3435

CHEZ GRANDMERE
24 Tinker Street
Woodstock
NY 12498
914 679 8140

THE COFFMAN ANTIQUES MARKET
Jenifer House Commons
Route 7
Great Barrington
MA 01230
413 528 9282

THE COUNTRY DINING ROOM
ANTIQUE
178 Main Street
Great Barrington
MA 01230
413 528 5050

BARBARA DAVIS
607 264 3673

DEAN & DELUCA
560 Broadway
New York
NY 10012
212 434 1691

THE DINING TABLE
306 E 61st Street
New York
NY 10021
212 755 2304

ELEISH-VAN BREEMS ANTIQUES
487 Main Street South
Woodbury
CT 06798
203 263 7030

FELISSIMO
10 W 56th Street
New York
NY 10019
212 956 4438

JAMES II GALLERIES
15 E 57th Street
New York
NY 10022
212 355 7040

MILLBROOK ANTIQUES CENTER
Franklin Avenue
Millbrook
NY 12545
914 677 3921

CHARLOTTE MOSS AND CO.
16 E 65th Street
New York
NY 10021
212 772 6244

OLDE ANTIQUES MARKET
Jenifer House Commons
Route 7
Great Barrington
MA 01230
413 528 1840

SIMON PEARCE
120 Wooster Street
New York
NY 10012
212 334 2393

PORTICO HOME
379 West Broadway
New York
NY 10012
212 941 7800

JAMES ROBINSON
480 Park Avenue
New York
NY 10022
212 752 6166

SCHWEITZER LINEN
1132 Madison Avenue
New York
NY 10028
1 800 554 6367

TAKASHIMAYA
693 Fifth Avenue
New York
NY 10022
1 800 753 2038

A LA VIEILLE RUSSIE
781 Fifth Avenue
New York
NY 10022
212 752 1727

VILLAGE ANTIQUES CENTER
Franklin Avenue
Millbrook
NY 12545
914 677 5160

WATERFORD WEDGWOOD
713 Madison Avenue
New York
NY 10021
212 759 0500

ZONA
97 Greene Street
New York
NY 10012
212 925 6750

FRANCE
Antiques and Decoration

ASTIER DE LA VILLATTE
5, rue de Médicis
75005 Paris
(0033) 01 43 26 31 25

BETJEMAN ET BARTON
23, boulevard Malesherbes
75008 Paris
(0033) 01 42 65 86 17

BLANC D'IVOIRE
4, rue Jacob
75007 Paris
(0033) 01 46 33 34 29

LE BON MARCHÉ
24, rue de Sèvres
75007 Paris
(0033) 01 44 39 80 00

CARAVANE
6, rue Pavée
75004 Paris
(0033) 01 44 61 04 20

ELSA C.
117, rue du Faubourg Saint-Antoine
75012 Paris
(0033) 01 44 75 78 85

L'HERBE VERTE
Galérie Vivienne
rue des Petits-Champs
75002 Paris
(0033) 01 40 20 45 09

JOCHEM KLUMPEN ANTIQUAIRE
'Le quai de la gare'
L'Isle sur Sorgue, Provence
(0033) 04 90 38 57 66

LAPARESSE EN DOUCE
97, rue du Bac
75007 Paris
(0033) 01 42 22 64 10

MAISON DE FAMILLE
10, place de la Madeleine
75008 Paris
(0033) 01 53 45 82 00

ÉDITH MÉZARD
Château de l'Ange
84220 Lumières
(0033) 04 90 72 36 41

MOKUBA
18, rue Montmartre
75001 Paris
(0033) 01 40 13 81 41

AU NOM DE LA ROSE
46, rue du Bac
75007 Paris
(0033) 01 42 22 22 12

MARIE PAPIER
26, rue Vavin
75006 Paris
(0033) 01 43 26 46 44

LE PASSÉ D'AUJOURD'HUI
43, rue du Cherche-Midi
75006 Paris
(0033) 01 42 22 41 21

PORTHAULT
18, avenue Montaigne
75008 Paris
(0033) 01 47 20 75 25

LE PRINCE JARDINIER
Jardins du Palais Royal
75001 Paris
(0033) 01 42 60 37 13

SENTOU GALERIE
26, boulevard Raspail
75007 Paris
(0033) 01 45 49 00 05

LA TUILE A LOUP
35, rue Daubenton
75005 Paris
(0033) 01 47 07 28 90

ITALY
Decoration

CRISTINA BELLINI
via San Maurilio, 20
Milano
(0039) 02 89 00 047

BELLORA
via Vincenzo Monti, 27
Milano
(0039) 02 43 90 092

BLANC DE BLANC
corso di Porta Romana, 6
Milano
(0039) 02 86 66 35

C & C
via della Spiga, 50
Milano
(0039) 02 78 02 57

COMPAGNIA DEI GIARDINI
via San Maurilio, 4
Milano
(0039) 02 72 02 19 77

LA COMPAGNIA DELL'ORIENTE
via Santa Marta, 10
Milano
(0039) 02 89 01 30 87

10 CORSO COMO
corso Como, 10
Milano
(0039) 02 29 00 26 74

ECLECTICA
corso Garibaldi, 3
Milano
(0039) 02 87 61 94

MIMMA GINI
via Santa Croce, 21
Milano
(0039) 02 89 40 07 22

PENELOPI 3
via Palermo, 1
Milano
(0039) 02 76 00 06 52

TAGLIETTI E COSTA
via San Marco, 34
Milano
(0039) 02 29 01 12 35

L'UTILE E IL DILETTEVOLE
via della Spiga, 46
Milano
(0039) 02 76 00 84 20

PICTURE CREDITS

Key: a=above, b=below, l=left, r=right, c=center

2 Designed by Lorraine Kirke; 3 Melanie Thornton's house in Gloucestershire; 4 Refurbishment and interior design by Chichi Meroni Fassio, Parnassus; 5 l Designer Barbara Davis' own house in upstate New York; 5 r Tita Bay's village house in Ramatuelle; 6 al Josephine Ryan's house in London; 6 ar & br Eleish-van Breems Antiques in Connecticut; 6 bl Lincoln Cato's house in Brighton; 7 Maria Vittoria Saibene's country house in Brunello on the lake of Varese; 12 l Lee Freund's Summerhouse in Southampton, New York; 13 r Eva Johnson's house in Suffolk, interiors designed by Eva Johnson; 14 & 15 r Designed by Lorraine Kirke; 15 l Lincoln Cato's house in Brighton; 16 a Nelly Guyot's house in Ramatuelle, France, styled by Nelly Guyot; 16 b Lincoln Cato's house in Brighton; 17 Eleish-van Breems Antiques in Connecticut; 18–19 Designer Barbara Davis' own house in upstate New York; 20 Marisa Cavalli's home in Milan; 21 Josephine Ryan's house in London; 22 a Melanie Thornton's house in Gloucestershire; 22 r & 23 Nelly Guyot's house in Ramatuelle, France, styled by Nelly Guyot; 24 Designed by Lorraine Kirke; 25 Refurbishment and interior design by Chichi Meroni Fassio, Parnassus; 26 l & br Josephine Ryan's house in London; 27 Lee Freund's Summerhouse in Southampton, New York; 28 Enrica Stabile's house in Le Thor, Provence; 29 Marisa Cavalli's home in Milan; 30–31 Enrica Stabile's house in Le Thor, Provence; 32 Josephine Ryan's house in London; 34–35 Enrica Stabile's house in Brunello; 36 Enrica Stabile's house in Le Thor, Provence; 38–39 Enrica Stabile's house in Brunello; 40–41 Enrica Stabile's house in Milan; 42–43 Designer Barbara Davis' own house in upstate New York; 44 al & bl Eva Johnson's house in Suffolk, interiors designed by Eva Johnson; 45 l Lincoln Cato's house in Brighton; 46 Marisa Cavalli's home in Milan; 47 Enrica Stabile's house in Milan; 48 & 49 l Marisa Cavalli's home in Milan; 49 b Eva Johnson's house in Suffolk, interiors designed by Eva Johnson; 50 b Eleish-van Breems Antiques in Connecticut; 50 r Enrica Stabile's house in Le Thor, Provence; 51 Nelly Guyot's house in Ramatuelle, France, styled by Nelly Guyot; 52 Ali Sharland's house in Gloucestershire; 53 l Eva Johnson's house in Suffolk, interiors designed by Eva Johnson; 54–55 Designer Barbara Davis' own house in upstate New York; 56 Melanie Thornton's house in Gloucestershire; 57 Tita Bay's village house in Ramatuelle; 58–59 Designer Barbara Davis' own house in upstate New York; 60–61 Lincoln Cato's house in Brighton; 62–63 Designer Barbara Davis' own house in upstate New York; 64 l Melanie Thornton's house in Gloucestershire; 64 r Lincoln Cato's house in Brighton; 65 Diane Bauer's house near Cotignac; 66–67 Eva Johnson's house in Suffolk, interiors designed by Eva Johnson; 68–69 Melanie Thornton's house in Gloucestershire; 70 Refurbishment and interior design by Chichi Meroni Fassio, Parnassus; 71 l Eleish-van Breems Antiques in Connecticut; 71 r Ali Sharland's house in Gloucestershire; 72–73 Tita Bay's village house in Ramatuelle; 74 l & 74–75 Nelly Guyot's house in Ramatuelle, France, styled by Nelly Guyot; 75 Diane Bauer's house near Cotignac; 76 Designed by Lorraine Kirke; 77 Lee Freund's Summerhouse in Southampton, New York; 78 Enrica Stabile's house in Brunello; 79 Ali Sharland's house in Gloucestershire; 80 & 81 r Josephine Ryan's house in London; 81 l Enrica Stabile's house in Milan; 82 a & bl Enrica Stabile's house in Brunello; 82 r Maria Vittoria Saibene's country house in Brunello on the lake of Varese; 83 Marisa Cavalli's home in Milan; 84 Ali Sharland's house in Gloucestershire; 86 Lincoln Cato's house in Brighton; 87 Diane Bauer's house near Cotignac; 88 Ali Sharland's house in Gloucestershire; 89 Melanie Thornton's house in Gloucestershire; 90–91 Enrica Stabile's house in Brunello; 92–93 Tita Bay's village house in Ramatuelle; 94–95 Refurbishment and interior design by Chichi Meroni Fassio, Parnassus; 96–97 Marisa Cavalli's home in Milan; 98–99 Eva Johnson's house in Suffolk, interiors designed by Eva Johnson; 100 Designed by Lorraine Kirke; 101 r Ali Sharland's house in Gloucestershire; 102 r Enrica Stabile's house in Le Thor, Provence; 103 l Marisa Cavalli's home in Milan; 103 r Diane Bauer's house near Cotignac; 104 Designer Barbara Davis' own house in upstate New York; 105 ar Enrica Stabile's house in Brunello; 105 br Josephine Ryan's house in London; 106–107 Designer Barbara Davis' own house in upstate New York; 108 a Enrica Stabile's house in Le Thor, Provence; 108 br & 109 Designed by Lorraine Kirke; 110 Enrica Stabile's house in Brunello; 111 Diane Bauer's house near Cotignac; 112 & 113 c Designed by Lorraine Kirke; 113 l & 114–115 Enrica Stabile's house in Le Thor, Provence; 116 Designed by Lorraine Kirke; 117 Melanie Thornton's house in Gloucestershire; 118–119 Eva

Johnson's house in Suffolk, interiors designed by Eva Johnson; 120–121 Designer Barbara Davis' own house in upstate New York; 122 Diane Bauer's house near Cotignac; 123 l Enrica Stabile's house in Brunello; 123 r Melanie Thornton's house in Gloucestershire; 124 Enrica Stabile's house in Brunello; 125 a & bl Refurbishment and interior design by Chichi Meroni Fassio, Parnassus; 125 r Diane Bauer's house near Cotignac; 126 l Enrica Stabile's house in Brunello; 126 r Refurbishment and interior design by Chichi Meroni Fassio, Parnassus; 127 Eva Johnson's house in Suffolk, interiors designed by Eva Johnson; 128–129 Enrica Stabile's house in Le Thor, Provence; 130 & 131 al Nelly Guyot's house in Ramatuelle, France, styled by Nelly Guyot; 131 ar Lincoln Cato's house in Brighton; 131 b Designer Barbara Davis' own house in upstate New York; 132 & 133 l Enrica Stabile's house in Brunello; 133 b Designer Barbara Davis' own house in upstate New York; 134–135 Diane Bauer's house near Cotignac; 136 Lee Freund's Summerhouse in Southampton, New York; 137 Designer Barbara Davis' own house in upstate New York; 138 Eleish-van Breems Antiques in Connecticut; 139 Designer Barbara Davis' own house in upstate New York; 140 & 141 Lee Freund's Summerhouse in Southampton, New York; 142 Designer Barbara Davis' own house in upstate New York; 143 Lee Freund's Summerhouse in Southampton, New York; 144 & endpapers Designer Barbara Davis' own house in upstate New York.

INTERIOR DESIGNERS WHOSE WORK IS FEATURED IN THIS BOOK

Tita Bay
Interior decorator
via Sudorno, 22D
24100 Bergamo
Italy
t. (0039) 03 52 58 384
Pages 5 r, 57, 72–73, 92–93

Lincoln Cato
t. (0044) 1273 325334
Pages 6 bl, 15 l, 16 b, 45 l, 60–61, 64 r, 86, 131 ar

Marisa Tadiotto Cavalli
via Solferino, 11
20121 Milano
Italy
t. (0039) 02 36 51 14 49
f. (0039) 02 29 00 18 60
m. (0039) 348 41 01 738
marisacavalli@hotmail.com
Pages 20, 28, 46, 48, 49 l, 83, 96–97, 102 l

Barbara Davis
t. 607 264 3673
Interior design; antique hand-dyed linen, wool, and silk textiles by the yard; soft furnishings and clothes to order.
Pages 5 l, 18–19, 42–43, 54–55, 58–59, 62–63, 104, 106–107, 120–121, 133 b, 137, 139, 142

Eleish-van Breems Antiques LLC
Thompson House
487 Main Street South
Woodbury
CT 06798
t. 203 263 7030/7031
f. 203 263 7032
evbantiq@wtco.net
www.evbantiques.com

Proprietors: Rhonda Eleish & Edie van Breems
Specializing in 18th- and 19th-century Scandinavian and Northern European antiques, garden elements, and decorative accessories, located in the historic Thompson House and garden.
Pages 6 ar & br, 17, 50 b, 71 l, 138

Nelly Guyot
Interior designer & photographic stylist
12, rue Marthe Edouard
92190 Meudon
France
Pages 16 a, 22 r, 23, 51, 74 l, 74–75, 130, 131 al

Eva Johnson
Interior designer
t. (0044) 1638 731 362
f. (0044) 1638 731 855
Distributor of TRIP-TRAP wood floor treatment products.
Pages 13 r, 44 al & bl, 49 b, 53 l, 66–67, 98–99, 118–119, 127

Parnassus
corso Porta Vittoria, 5
Milan
Italy
t. (0039) 02 78 11 07
Pages 4, 25, 70, 94–95, 125 a & bl, 126 r

Sharland & Lewis
52 Long Street
Tetbury
Gloucestershire GL8 8AQ
t. (0044) 1666 500354
www.sharlandandlewis.com
Pages 52, 71 r, 79, 84, 88, 101 r

Enrica Stabile
via della Spiga, 46
Milan
Italy
t. (0039) 02 76 00 84 20
e.stabile@enricastabile.com
www.enricastabile.com
Antiques dealer, interior decorator, and photographic stylist.
Pages 28, 30–31, 34–35, 36, 38–39, 40–41, 47, 50 r, 78, 81 l, 82 a & bl, 90–91, 102 r, 105 ar, 108 a, 110, 113 l, 114–115, 123 l, 124, 126 l, 128–129, 132, 133 l

INDEX

ACKNOWLEDGMENTS

Thank you to Gabriella Le Grazie who gave me a second chance after *Open Air Living* with this wonderful book, so very close to my spirit. Thank you to Julia Watson, who beautifully expressed through words what I tried to express through pictures. And a thousand thank yous to Chris Drake who, as always, patient, competent, and dedicated, put up with me and my whimsical character and with unflagging good humor again produced superb photographs. Thank you to all the fantastic people who very generously shared their houses with us: Diane Bauer, Tita Bay, Jill and Lincoln Cato, Marisa Cavalli, Barbara Davis, Nelly Guyot, Rhonda Eleish, Eva Johnson, Lorraine Kirke, Giulana & Federico Magnifico, Maria Cristina Meroni Fassio, Lee Freund, Josephine Ryan, Toia Saibene, Ali Sharland, Melanie Thornton, Elisabeth van Breems. Thank you to Alberto Bellinzona, a hardworking, creative, resourceful, and very capable assistant. Thank you to Clare Double, to Vicky Holmes, and the team at RPS who smoothed, rushed ... and eventually produced *Comfortable Country*.